This Book Belongs To

love

IT'S YOUR BIRTHDAY!

what is your birthdate?

_____

What was your full name at birth?

_____

Were you named after a relative or someone else of significance?

_____

_____

In what city were you born?

_____

what was your height(length) and weight at birth?

_____

Were you born in a hospital?If not, where?

_____

_____

What were your first words?

_____

_____

IT'S YOUR BIRTHDAY!

How old were your parents when you were born?

_____

How many siblings do you have?

_____

If you have siblings,were you the oldest,middle,or youngest child?

_____

_____

How did your parents describe you as a baby?

_____

_____

_____

_____

_____

IT'S YOUR BIRTHDAY!

what story have you been told about the day you were born?

_____

_____

_____

_____

_____

_____

_____

_____

_____

_____

_____

_____

_____

_____

_____

_____

IT'S YOUR BIRTHDAY!

What is a favourite childhood memory?

_____

_____

_____

_____

_____

_____

_____

_____

_____

_____

_____

_____

_____

Tell Me About Your Family

what were your parent's name? _____

_____

_____

_____

_____

_____

what were your parent's professions? _____

_____

_____

_____

_____

_____

_____

_____

_____

Tell Me About Your Family

What were your parents like?

_____

_____

_____

_____

_____

_____

_____

_____

_____

_____

_____

_____

_____

_____

How did you meet Mom/Dad?

_____

_____

_____

_____

_____

_____

_____

_____

_____

_____

_____

_____

_____

_____

_____

_____

_____

Tell me about the day I was born.

What's the hardest thing about raising children?

What did you want to be when you were growing up?

What tells you when a child is responsible enough to trust a lot?

What is one thing you know to be true?

_____

_____

_____

_____

_____

_____

_____

_____

_____

_____

_____

_____

_____

_____

_____

_____

What were you going to name me if I was the opposite sex?

_____

_____

_____

_____

_____

_____

_____

_____

_____

_____

_____

_____

_____

_____

_____

_____

What was your first car?

_____

_____

_____

_____

_____

What's your fondest memory in your first car?

_____

_____

_____

_____

_____

_____

_____

_____

_____

_____

_____

How often do you go over the speed limit?

Were you considered popular in middle school or high school? Why or why not?

_____

_____

_____

_____

_____

_____

_____

_____

_____

_____

_____

_____

_____

_____

_____

_____

Did you have big fights with your mom when you were growing up?

_____

_____

_____

_____

_____

_____

_____

If so, what were they usually about?   _____

_____

_____

_____

_____

_____

_____

_____

_____

Did you have big fights with your dad when you were growing up?

_____

_____

_____

_____

_____

_____

_____

If so, what were they usually about? _____

_____

_____

_____

_____

_____

_____

_____

_____

Did you ever get arrested for anything?

_____

_____

_____

_____

_____

_____

_____

_____

If not, did you ever do anything you should have gotten in trouble for if anyone had found out?

_____

_____

_____

_____

_____

_____

_____

_____

If you could do any job in the world, besides the one you are doing now, what would it be?

What kinds of things get you angriest? Why?

_____

_____

_____

_____

_____

_____

_____

_____

_____

_____

_____

_____

_____

_____

_____

_____

When, if ever, do you think it's okay to tell a lie?

How old do you think you look? Why?

How did you and Mom/Dad meet?

_____

_____

_____

_____

_____

_____

_____

_____

_____

_____

_____

_____

_____

_____

_____

_____

How old are you in your dreams? What are you doing?

What was your favorite pet when you were a kid?

_____

_____

_____

_____

_____

_____

_____

_____

_____

_____

_____

_____

_____

_____

_____

_____

Why did your parents give you your name?

What is your favorite joke? Why?

_____

_____

_____

_____

_____

_____

_____

_____

_____

_____

_____

_____

_____

_____

_____

_____

What was the best thing I ever gave you?

_____

_____

_____

_____

_____

_____

_____

_____

_____

_____

_____

_____

_____

_____

_____

_____

_____

_____

Who was your best friend in high school and what was the best thing about this person?

_____

_____

_____

_____

_____

_____

_____

_____

_____

_____

_____

_____

_____

_____

_____

_____

_____

If you could afford any car in the world, what would it be?

Do you think you have any prejudices? What would they be?

_____

_____

_____

_____

_____

_____

_____

_____

_____

_____

_____

_____

_____

_____

_____

_____

Is there any experience that you have not had that you regret not having?

_____

_____

_____

_____

_____

_____

_____

_____

_____

_____

_____

_____

_____

_____

_____

_____

What qualities do you most respect in a woman? In a man?

_____

_____

_____

_____

_____

_____

_____

_____

_____

_____

_____

_____

_____

_____

_____

_____

Is it okay for someone who is twenty-two to marry someone who is forty or fifty? Why or why not?

How would people who knew you in middle school describe you then?

_____

_____

_____

_____

_____

_____

_____

_____

_____

_____

_____

_____

_____

_____

_____

How would people who knew you in high school describe you?

_____

_____

_____

_____

_____

_____

_____

_____

_____

_____

_____

_____

_____

_____

_____

_____

_____

How would you describe Dad/Mom the first time you saw him/her?

_____

_____

_____

_____

_____

_____

_____

_____

_____

_____

_____

_____

_____

_____

_____

What makes a good friend?

How do you tell when someone is lying?

What do you think is your worst bad habit?

Have you ever done something brave? If so, did you regret it?

_____

_____

_____

_____

_____

_____

_____

_____

_____

_____

_____

_____

_____

_____

_____

What's the worst dream you can remember?

_____

_____

_____

_____

_____

_____

_____

_____

_____

_____

_____

_____

_____

_____

_____

_____

_____

How much money does a person need to have a good life?

_____

_____

_____

_____

_____

_____

_____

_____

_____

_____

_____

_____

_____

_____

_____

Did you ever wish you didn't have children? If so, what made you think that?

_____

_____

_____

_____

_____

_____

_____

_____

_____

_____

_____

_____

_____

_____

_____

_____

_____

Would you rather be famous, or make a lot of money? Why?

Have you ever been hit? If so, tell me what happened.

What is the worst thing that your parents ever said to you?

_____

_____

_____

_____

_____

_____

_____

_____

_____

_____

_____

_____

_____

_____

_____

_____

What makes you lose your temper with me?

_____

_____

_____

_____

_____

_____

_____

_____

_____

_____

_____

_____

_____

_____

_____

_____

What age group of kids do you think you are best with: babies, middle-school, or high school?

_____

_____

_____

_____

_____

_____

_____

_____

_____

_____

_____

_____

_____

_____

_____

_____

_____

_____

What have you said to me that you wish you hadn't?

_____

_____

_____

_____

_____

_____

_____

_____

_____

_____

_____

_____

_____

_____

_____

_____

_____

_____

Did kids ever make fun of you for any reason? What do you remember best?

_____

_____

_____

_____

_____

_____

_____

_____

_____

_____

_____

_____

_____

_____

_____

Would you get upset if I wanted to live in another country when I was grown up? Why or why not?

There are two kinds of weddings: big fancy ones and small private ones. Which do you like?

_____

_____

_____

_____

_____

_____

_____

_____

_____

_____

_____

_____

_____

_____

_____

_____

Did you ever run away from home? If you did, why did you do it?

If you didn't, did you ever think about it? Do you remember what the issue was?

_____

_____

_____

_____

_____

_____

_____

_____

_____

_____

_____

_____

_____

_____

_____

_____

What are your all-time favorite movies? Why?

What kinds of things make you sad?

_____

_____

_____

_____

_____

_____

_____

_____

_____

_____

_____

_____

_____

_____

_____

If you could be any female sports star, who would you be?

_____

_____

_____

_____

_____

_____

_____

_____

_____

_____

_____

_____

_____

_____

_____

_____

_____

_____

Did you ever get jealous of someone?

_____

_____

_____

_____

_____

_____

_____

_____

_____

_____

_____

_____

_____

_____

_____

_____

Do you think people are born intelligent, or can they be made intelligent?

Would you admit to me if you were afraid of something?

Do you think there should be a death penalty for murder, or should the worst possible punishment be life in prison? Tell me why you have this opinion.

_____

_____

_____

_____

_____

_____

_____

_____

_____

_____

_____

_____

_____

_____

_____

_____

_____

_____

Do you think it is ok for a man to be the person who stays home with the kids instead of the woman? Why or why not?

_____

_____

_____

_____

_____

_____

_____

_____

_____

_____

_____

_____

_____

_____

_____

_____

If you won the lottery, what would you do with the money?

_____

_____

_____

_____

_____

_____

_____

_____

_____

_____

_____

_____

_____

_____

_____

_____

_____

_____

What makes you like one of my friends? What would make you dislike one of my friends?

_____

_____

_____

_____

_____

_____

_____

_____

_____

_____

_____

_____

_____

_____

_____

_____

Have you ever thought of adopting a child? Why or why not?

_____

_____

_____

_____

_____

_____

_____

_____

_____

_____

_____

_____

_____

_____

_____

_____

_____

_____

What did you get in trouble for when you were a kid?

_____

_____

_____

_____

_____

_____

_____

_____

_____

_____

_____

_____

_____

_____

_____

Did you ever have a teacher who picked on you?

What was the most embarrassing thing that ever happened to you?

Is my personality the same now as it was when I was younger?
Tell me how I am the same or different.

_____

_____

_____

_____

_____

_____

_____

_____

_____

_____

_____

_____

_____

_____

_____

_____

_____

Why is it such a big deal for rooms to be clean?

_____

_____

_____

_____

_____

_____

_____

_____

_____

_____

_____

_____

_____

_____

Why do you care if I fight with my brothers or sisters or wrestle with my friends?

_____

_____

_____

_____

_____

_____

_____

_____

_____

_____

_____

_____

_____

_____

_____

_____

_____

_____

_____

How often do you think you scream at me? Why do you think people scream?

_____

_____

_____

_____

_____

_____

_____

_____

_____

_____

_____

_____

_____

_____

_____

_____

How would you feel if I changed my first name? Last name?

What really gives you the creeps?

Did you like middle school? High school? Why or why not?

_____

_____

_____

_____

_____

_____

_____

_____

_____

_____

_____

_____

_____

_____

_____

_____

_____

In what ways do you think you are similar to me?

_____

_____

_____

_____

_____

_____

_____

_____

_____

_____

_____

_____

_____

_____

In what ways do you think you are different from me?

_____

_____

_____

_____

_____

_____

_____

_____

_____

_____

_____

_____

_____

_____

_____

_____

What was your biggest disappointment when you were a kid?

What is the thing you wanted most that you haven't gotten?

_____

_____

_____

_____

_____

_____

_____

_____

_____

_____

_____

_____

_____

_____

_____

_____

Who was the best teacher you ever had? And the worst? Why?

_____

_____

_____

_____

_____

_____

_____

_____

_____

_____

_____

_____

_____

_____

_____

_____

What toy did you want when you were a kid that you never got?

_____

_____

_____

_____

_____

_____

_____

_____

_____

_____

_____

_____

_____

_____

_____

_____

What toy did you want when you were a kid that you never got?

_____

_____

_____

_____

_____

_____

_____

_____

_____

_____

_____

_____

_____

_____

_____

_____

What were the three happiest moments in your life so far?

_____

_____

_____

_____

_____

_____

_____

_____

_____

_____

_____

_____

_____

_____

_____

_____

What things do we have now that you didn't have when you were growing up?

_____

_____

_____

_____

_____

_____

_____

_____

_____

_____

_____

_____

_____

_____

What kinds of things did your mom and dad do with you that you have tried to do differently with us?

_____

_____

_____

_____

_____

_____

_____

_____

_____

_____

_____

_____

_____

_____

_____

_____

_____

Did you have a nickname in middle school or high school?
If so, what was it and how did you get it?

_____

_____

_____

_____

_____

_____

_____

_____

_____

_____

_____

_____

_____

_____

_____

_____

When you were a kid, did you have a favorite hiding place?

_____

_____

_____

_____

_____

_____

_____

_____

_____

_____

_____

_____

_____

_____

_____

_____

When you were a kid, did you ever belong to a club?
If you did, how many people became a member and what did you do together?

_____

_____

_____

_____

_____

_____

_____

_____

_____

_____

_____

_____

_____

_____

_____

_____

What's the hardest/easiest thing about being an adult?

If your life was a reality show, what would it be called?

_____

_____

_____

_____

_____

_____

_____

_____

_____

_____

_____

_____

_____

_____

What do you like/dislike about your generation?

_____

_____

_____

_____

_____

_____

_____

_____

_____

_____

_____

_____

_____

_____

_____

_____

_____

Who is someone you admire? Why?

_____

_____

_____

_____

_____

_____

_____

_____

_____

_____

_____

_____

_____

_____

_____

_____

Do you think money can buy happiness?

Were your parents strict? Was your Mom or Dad the strictest?

_____

_____

_____

_____

_____

_____

_____

_____

_____

_____

_____

_____

_____

_____

_____

What are the 3 happiest times in your life?

_____

_____

_____

_____

_____

_____

_____

_____

_____

_____

_____

_____

_____

_____

_____

_____

_____

What is your dream job?

_____

_____

_____

_____

_____

_____

_____

_____

_____

_____

_____

_____

_____

_____

_____

_____

Made in the USA
Monee, IL
06 October 2023

44103693R00057